Spelling Mastery
Level C
Workbook

Robert Dixon

Siegfried Engelmann

D1476025

SRA McGraw-Hill

Columbus, Ohio

A Division of The **McGraw·Hill** *Companies*

Photo Credits
Cover, ©James Wells/Tony Stone Images; Back Cover (inset),
©Carol Havens/Tony Stone Images.

SRA/McGraw-Hill

*A Division of The **McGraw·Hill** Companies*

Send all inquiries to:
SRA/McGraw-Hill
8787 Orion Place
Columbus, OH 43240-4027

Printed in the United States of America.

ISBN 0-02-687625-6

12 WEB 06

LESSON 1

PART A

green   keep   need   see   street   beetle   weed

PART B

I thought he was through.

PART C

friends   enough   wonder   quiet   listen

PART D

1. book   •   •   _ _ _ _ _
2. look   •   •   _ _ _ d
3. good   •   •   b _ _ _
4. stood   •   •   t _ _ _
5. took   •   •   _ _ _ _

PART E

These words are in the puzzle.
Circle 7 or more of the words.

beetle	friends	need
enough	blue	shut
should	talk	put
high	home	have

```
e  b  h  t  a  l  k
s  n  e  e  d  e  e
f  r  i  e  n  d  s
s  s  h  n  t  b  n
h  s  h  o  u  l  d
o  i  p  u  t  u  e
m  n  g  g  t  e  e
e  s  h  h  a  v  e
```

1

LESSON 2

PART A

1. _____   4. _____

2. _____   5. _____

3. _____   6. _____

PART B

1. _ h e _ _   4. _ _ _ _ e _

2. _ o u _ _   5. _ a _ _

3. _ _ _ _ l e

PART C

_ _ _ o u g h _   _ _ _ a _ _ _ _ o u g h .

_____

PART D

Figure out the words in the second column and write them.
Then draw lines to the same words in the first column.

1. come	•	• _ _ n _
2. shove	•	• _ _ _ _
3. none	•	d _ _ _ _
4. done	•	c _ _ _ _
5. some	•	_ _ m _
6. love	•	_ _ _ _ _

2

These words are in the puzzle.
Circle 7 or more of the words.

wonder	thought	listen
enough	stood	south
over	even	take
dog	wood	could

t	a	k	e	s	c	l
t	h	w	n	t	o	i
s	t	o	o	d	u	s
o	e	n	u	o	l	t
u	v	d	g	g	d	e
t	e	e	h	e	h	n
h	n	r	r	n	o	t

LESSON 3

PART A

1. _____
2. _____
3. _____
4. _____

5. _____
6. _____
7. _____
8. _____

PART B

_____ did you _____ Sandy?

PART C

_ __ou___ __ ___ _____gh.

_____

PART D

I thout she was dunn.

Meny books are good.

PART E

Figure out the words in the second column and write them.
Then draw lines to the same words in the first column.

1. little •
2. were •
3. better •
4. should •
5. shove •

• _ _ _ u l _
• _ _ t t _ _
• _ _ o _ _
• _ _ _ _ e _
• _ _ _ _

4

These words are in the puzzle.
Circle 7 or more of the words.

through	race	help
could	street	gone
oats	nose	should
cell	where	reach

```
s  w  h  e  r  e  s
t  h  r  o  u  g  h
r  c  e  a  t  o  o
e  e  o  l  c  n  u
e  l  a  u  p  e  l
t  l  t  c  l  e  d
n  o  s  e  h  d  d
```

5

LESSON 4

PART A

_____

PART B

1. _____   5. _____

2. _____   6. _____

3. _____   7. _____

4. _____   8. _____

PART C

Cross out the misspelled words in these sentences.
Then write the words correctly above the crossed-out words.

I think she is throo.

Do you have enuf frends?

PART D

Write each of these words in a box.

were	scold	should	book
would	green	thought	better
south	good	over	little
many	where	listen	meet

Lesson 5 is a test lesson. There is no worksheet.

6

LESSON 6

PART A

1. _____   6. _____

2. _____   7. _____

3. _____   8. _____

4. _____   9. _____

5. _____   10. _____

PART B

He writes better than he talks.

_____

PART C

Cross out the misspelled words in these sentences.
Then write the words correctly above the crossed-out words.

I thawt she was throo.

Lissen to your frend.

PART D

Figure out the words in the second column and write them.
Then draw lines to the same words in the first column.

1. shove   •   • _ _ _ _
2. little   •   • s h _ _ _ _ _
3. should   •   • _ _ _ _ _ _
4. many   •   • s h _ _ _
5. some   •   • _ _ _ _ l _
6. wonder   •   • _ a _ _

7

LESSON 7

PART A

1. might   3. right   5. light

2. flight   4. tight   6. bright

PART B

1. _____   5. _____

2. _____   6. _____

3. _____   7. _____

4. _____   8. _____

PART C

__ _r i _ es ___te_ ____ __ _a l k_.

_____

PART D

1. _____

2. _____

PART E

Figure out each word and write it in the blank below.

    tseert   tillet   tebret   ghourth

1. _____ 2. _____ 3. _____ 4. _____

8

LESSON 8

PART A

1. fight   2. light   3. night

PART B

1. _____

2. _____

PART C

1. _____   4. _____

2. _____   5. _____

3. _____   6. _____

PART D

__ __ r i e_ ____e_ ____ __ _a l__.

_____

PART E

Cross out the misspelled words in these sentences.
Then write the words correctly above the crossed-out words.

We nede a lite on our strete.

His friends are queit.

9

LESSON 9

PART A

__ __ r i___ _____ ____ __ _____.

_____

PART B

1. _____   5. _____

2. _____   6. _____

3. _____   7. _____

4. _____   8. _____

PART C

1. _____

2. _____

• •

Lesson 10 is a test lesson. There is no worksheet.

LESSON 11

PART A

1. _____   4. _____

2. _____   5. _____

3. _____   6. _____

PART B

__ __ __ __ __ __ __ __ __ __ __ __ __ __ __ __ __ __ __ __ __ __ __ __ __ .

_____

PART C

Figure out the words in the second column and write them.
Then draw lines to the same words in the first column.

1. listen   •   • _ h _ _ _ _ _

2. little   •   • _ _ _ _ _ e

3. fright   •   • _ _ _ _ _ _

4. flight   •   • _ _ _ t _ _

5. thought •   • _ l _ _ _ _

6. through •   • _ _ _ _ g _ _

PART D

These words are in the puzzle.
Circle 7 or more of the words.

writes   fright   high

tight   grin   fight

steep   shot

t	f	f	f	h	g	r
i	w	r	i	t	e	s
g	r	i	n	g	o	h
h	i	g	h	i	h	o
t	o	h	t	h	t	t
s	s	t	e	e	p	t

11

LESSON 12

© SRA/McGraw-Hill. All rights reserved.

PART A

1. _____   4. _____

2. _____   5. _____

3. _____   6. _____

PART B

My grandmother ate bananas for breakfast.

_____

_____

PART C

1. _____

2. _____

PART D

Cross out the misspelled words in these sentences.
Then write the words correctly above the crossed-out words.

That lite has turned grene.

She rites enuf.

You shoud eat some meet.

12

LESSON **13**

PART A

1. _____   5. _____

2. _____   6. _____

3. _____   7. _____

4. _____   8. _____

PART B

1. _____   4. _____

2. _____   5. _____

3. _____   6. _____

PART C

_y _r_nd_o__er __e _a_ana_
_or b_eak_as_.

_____

_____

PART D

Figure out each word and write it in the blank below.

     hwy   ifdesrn   gotuhht

1. _____   2. _____   3. _____

     ewehr   itslne   mose

4. _____   5. _____   6. _____

LESSON 14

PART A

1. _____ 5. _____
2. _____ 6. _____
3. _____ 7. _____
4. _____ 8. _____

PART B

__ ___nd_o_e_ __e _a_a_as
_o_ __ea__as_.

_____

_____

PART C

Figure out the words in the second column and write them.
Then draw lines to the same words in the first column.

1. bright •   • _ l _ _ _ _
2. flight •   • _ _ _
3. sight •   • _ _ _ _ _ _
4. writes •   • s _ _ _
5. shy   •   • _ _ _ t _ _
6. why   •   • _ _ _ _ _

....

Lesson 15 is a test lesson. There is no worksheet.

14

LESSON 16

PART A

1. _____   3. _____
2. _____   4. _____

PART B

_ _   _ _ _ n _ _ _ _ _ e _   _ _   _ a _ a _ a _
_ _ _   _ _ _ a _ _ _ _ .

_____

_____

PART C

1. _____   5. _____
2. _____   6. _____
3. _____   7. _____
4. _____   8. _____

PART D

Draw a line from each word to its clue.

1. meat •   • Please _____ me after school.

2. meet •   • had some food

3. ate   •   • something to eat

4. for   •   • I had an apple _____ a snack.

LESSON 17

1. _____   5. _____

2. _____   6. _____

3. _____   7. _____

4. _____

PART B

`__   _____   __   _____`

`___   _____.`

_____

_____

PART C

Write each of these words in a box.

| why | good | green | than | light | writes | keep | listen |
| quiet | shy | sight | meat | should | thought | book | high |

16

Draw a line from each word to its clue.

1. right   •

2. meat   •

3. through   •

4. meet   •

5. ate   •

• We are _____ with the lesson.

• We _____ dinner early.

• a type of food

• correct

• Let's _____ after school.

LESSON 18

PART A

1. _____   5. _____
2. _____   6. _____
3. _____   7. _____
4. _____

PART B

She didn't listen to anybody.

_____

PART C

1. _____
2. _____

PART D

Cross out the misspelled words in these sentences.
Then write the words correctly above the crossed-out words.

Her brekfast was gud.

They ate bananes every nite.

PART E

Figure out each word and write it in the blank below.

    pate   ghirt   egrne   yhs

1. _____   2. _____   3. _____   4. _____

18

LESSON 19

PART A

1. _____   5. _____
2. _____   6. _____
3. _____   7. _____
4. _____   8. _____

PART B

___ ___n't ___te_ __ __ybo_y.

_____

PART C

These words are in the puzzle.
Circle 7 or more of the words.

shape   escape   enough
than   chain   street
gentle   even   thing

e	s	c	a	p	e
n	t	h	a	n	v
o	r	a	a	t	e
u	e	i	s	p	n
g	e	n	t	l	e
h	t	h	i	n	g

Lesson 20 is a test lesson. There is no worksheet.

19

LESSON 21

PART A

1. _____   4. _____

2. _____   5. _____

3. _____

PART B

___ ___n't __s___ __ ___bo__.

_____

PART C

1. _____

2. _____

PART D

Draw a line from each word to its clue.

1. through •   • putting words on paper

2. write •   • Stay _____ the show.

3. meat •   • We _____ bananas.

4. for •   • I thought he was _____ .

5. meet •   • get together

6. ate •   • a type of food

20

LESSON 22

PART A

1. _____   4. _____

2. _____   5. _____

3. _____

PART B

___ ___n't _is___ __ ___bo__.

_____

PART C

1. _____   5. _____

2. _____   6. _____

3. _____   7. _____

4. _____   8. _____

PART D

Figure out the words in the second column and write them.
Then draw lines to the same words in the first column.

1. escape •   • _ _ _ _ t

2. didn't •   • d _ _ _ _

3. today   •   • _ _ _ n' _

4. grape   •   • _ _ d _ _

5. drape   •   • _ _ _ _ _

6. might   •   • _ h _ _ _

7. quiet   •   • _ _ _ h _

8. shove   •   • _ _ _ _ _

21

LESSON 23

PART A

1. _____   4. _____

2. _____   5. _____

3. _____   6. _____

PART B

_ _ _   _ _ _ _ _   _ _ _ _ _ _   _ _   _ _ _ _ _ _ _ .

_____

PART C

Write each of these words in a box.

porch   flight   than   ate   through   writes   away   tape
say   corn   shape   green   quiet   sport   shy   meat

PART D

Cross out the misspelled words in these sentences.
Then write the words correctly above the crossed-out words.

My granmother has gud frends.

We ate sum litle bananes.

LESSON 24

PART A

1. _____   4. _____

2. _____   5. _____

3. _____   6. _____

PART B

1. _____

2. _____

PART C

Figure out each word and write it in the blank below.

psrot   aydto   lyf   iltgh

1. _____   2. _____   3. _____   4. _____

PART D

Draw a line from each word to its clue.

1. meat   •   • We thought she was _____ .

2. through   •   • Dad _____ a banana.

3. right   •   • I asked _____ a fork.

4. for   •   • correct

5. ate   •   • a type of food

· ·

Lesson 25 is a test lesson. There is no worksheet.

23

LESSON 26

PART A

1. _____   5. _____
2. _____   6. _____
3. _____   7. _____
4. _____   8. _____

PART B

1. _____
2. _____

PART C

Cross out the misspelled words in these sentences.
Then write the words correctly above the crossed-out words.

We will be throuh at noon.

I had gud food for brekfast.

The moon was brite last nite.

PART D

Figure out the words in the second column and write them.
Then draw lines to the same words in the first column.

1. coop   •   • _ _ _ _ _
2. boot   •   • _ _ _ p
3. fool   •   • f _ _ _
4. food   •   • _ r _ _ _
5. shape •   • _ _ _ _
6. grape •   • _ _ _ l

24

LESSON 27

PART A

want   these   which   them   brush   think

PART B

1. _____
2. _____
3. _____
4. _____

5. _____
6. _____
7. _____
8. _____

PART C

Figure out each word and write it in the blank below.

ghtti   ttille   rpcho   tnaw

1. _____   2. _____   3. _____   4. _____

PART D

Draw a line from each word to its clue.

1. meet •
2. meat •
3. for •
4. ate •
5. through •

• Thank you _____ the food.

• I will _____ you soon.

• We are _____ for the day.

• beef, pork, chicken

• Our grandmother _____ breakfast.

25

LESSON 28

PART A

-ack   -eck   -ick   -ock   -uck

PART B

1. _____

2. _____

PART C

1. _____   4. _____

2. _____   5. _____

3. _____   6. _____

PART D

Cross out the misspelled words in these sentences.
Then write the words correctly above the crossed-out words.

He did'nt play with anybudy.

Lissen to that old taip.

PART E

Figure out each word and write it in the blank below.

      heset   moobl   temh   etiqu

1. _____   2. _____   3. _____   4. _____

26

LESSON 29

PART A

-ack   -eck   -ick   -ock   -uck

PART B

1. _____   4. _____

2. _____   5. _____

3. _____

PART C

1. _____

2. _____

PART D

Write each of these words in a box.

| think | bloom | brush | escape | didn't | sport | them | shape |
| room | which | anybody | why | these | porch | want | light |

....

Lesson 30 is a test lesson. There is no worksheet.

27

LESSON 31

-ack   -eck   -ick   -ock   -uck

PART **B**

I believe he lost every race.

_____

PART **C**

1. _ r u _ _   4. _ _ l _
2. s _ _ _ l   5. _ o _ _ e _
3. _ o _ _

PART **D**

I want you to _____ my _____.

PART **E**

1. _____   6. _____
2. _____   7. _____
3. _____   8. _____
4. _____   9. _____
5. _____

28

PART F

Cross out the misspelled words in these sentences.
Then write the words correctly above the crossed-out words.

I feel a litle bettor.

Your hoam is very quiut.

PART G

These words are in the puzzle.
Circle 7 or more of the words.

told	talks	better
able	after	above
vote	feel	anybody
neat	lie	light

```
a  t  a  l  k  s  a
a  n  n  f  i  f  a
b  b  e  t  t  e  r
o  t  l  a  o  e  e
v  o  t  e  t  l  r
e  l  i  g  h  t  d
a  n  y  b  o  d  y
```

LESSON 32

PART A

1. p<u>a</u>ck   3. l<u>u</u>ck   5. l<u>o</u>ck   7. b<u>a</u>ck   9. st<u>a</u>ck
2. k<u>i</u>ck   4. n<u>e</u>ck   6. s<u>i</u>ck   8. r<u>o</u>ck   10. th<u>i</u>ck

PART B

_ _e_i e_ _ _ _ _o_ _ _ _e_y _ _c e.

_____

PART C

1. _____   5. _____
2. _____   6. _____
3. _____   7. _____
4. _____   8. _____

PART D

I _____ like to _____ your brother.

PART E

Figure out each word and write it in the blank below.

erewh   ghouthr   woernd   iequt

1. _____ 2. _____ 3. _____ 4. _____

30

Figure out the words in the second column and write them.
Then draw lines to the same words in the first column.

1. neck •   • _ _ _ c _

2. these •   • _ e _ _

3. then •   • _ _ _ k

4. pack •   • w _ _ _

5. thick •   • _ _ e _ _

6. want •   • _ h _ _

LESSON 33

PART A

1. _____   5. _____
2. _____   6. _____
3. _____   7. _____
4. _____   8. _____

PART B

_ _ _ _ i e _ _   _ _   _ _ _ _   _ _ e _ y   _ _ c _.

_____

PART C

Figure out each word and write it in the blank below.

namy   ckpa   iendfr   verye

1. _____   2. _____   3. _____   4. _____

PART D

Cross out the misspelled words in these sentences.
Then write the words correctly above the crossed-out words.

I beleeve they are thru.

Do you think this is enogh?

32

Figure out the words in the second column and write them.
Then draw lines to the same words in the first column.

1. kick   •   • _ _ _ _ _ _

2. than   •   • _ i _ _ _

3. where   •   • _ _ _ _ e _

4. sack   •   • _ h _ _

5. little   •   • _ a _ _

6. wonder   •   • _ _ _ _ _

LESSON 34

PART A

-adge -edge -idge -odge -udge

PART B

1. _____ 4. _____

2. _____ 5. _____

3. _____ 6. _____

PART C

Did you _____ the dog _____ bark?

PART D

1. _____

2. _____

PART E

Figure out each word and write it in the blank below.

   kooc   cera   doulw   erbett

1. _____ 2. _____ 3. _____ 4. _____

Lesson 35 is a test lesson. There is no worksheet.

34

LESSON 36

PART A

-adge   -edge   -idge   -odge   -udge

PART B

1. _____   5. _____

2. _____   6. _____

3. _____   7. _____

4. _____   8. _____

PART C

People watched from the other building.

_____

_____

PART D

I _____ like some _____, please.

PART E

1. _ _ _ i _ _ _   4. _ _ e _ _

2. _ _ _ _ u _ _   5. _ _ a _ _

3. _ o _ _ _ _

PART F

Figure out each word and write it in the blank below.

     peolpe   inkth   aylp   ownbr

1. _____   2. _____   3. _____   4. _____

LESSON 37

PART A

-adge   -edge   -idge   -odge   -udge

PART B

1. _____
2. _____
3. _____
4. _____
5. _____
6. _____

PART C

_eo_le _atch__ __o_ ___
o__e_ _uil____.

_____

_____

PART D

1. _____
2. _____

PART E

Figure out the words in the second column and write them.
Then draw lines to the same words in the first column.

1. blue   •   • _ _ _ _
2. beetle   •   • _ _ r _
3. port   •   • _ o _ _
4. shock   •   • _ _ _ _ _
5. some   •   • _ _ e _ _
6. these   •   • _ _ _ _ k

36

LESSON 38

PART A

1. _____   5. _____

2. _____   6. _____

3. _____   7. _____

4. _____   8. _____

PART B

_ _ o _ _ _   _ _ t _ _ _ _   _ _ o _   _ _ _
o _ _ _ _   _ u i _ _ _ _ _ .

_____

_____

PART C

1. <u>ba</u>dge   4. <u>ju</u>dge   7. h<u>e</u>dge

2. br<u>i</u>dge   5. l<u>e</u>dge   8. r<u>i</u>dge

3. d<u>o</u>dge   6. f<u>u</u>dge   9. pl<u>e</u>dge

PART D

1. _____

2. _____

PART E

Draw a line from each word to its clue.

1. meat   •   •   Did you _____ the train?

2. meet   •   •   Most people _____ like this show.

3. wood   •   •   something to eat

4. would •   •   something to build with

37

These words are in the puzzle.
Circle 7 or more of the words.

think	silk	park
judge	stop	grape
shop	cool	build
shore	leash	people

```
t  s  s  h  h  k
l  t  h  i  n  k
e  c  o  o  l  o
a  b  p  a  r  k
s  j  u  d  g  e
h  t  o  i  o  o
p  e  o  p  l  e
g  r  a  p  e  d
```

LESSON 39

PART A

1. _____
2. _____
3. _____
4. _____

5. _____
6. _____
7. _____
8. _____

PART B

1. _____
2. _____
3. _____
4. _____

5. _____
6. _____
7. _____
8. _____

PART C

1. _____
2. _____
3. _____

PART D

Draw a line from each word to its clue.

1. would •

2. meat •

3. wood •

4. meet •

5. through •

• comes from cattle

• I'll _____ you at noon.

• We walked _____ the room.

• comes from trees

• I _____ not say that.

39

Figure out each word and write it in the blank below.

thorau   ingldbui   chrea   ntoip

1. _____ 2. _____ 3. _____ 4. _____

Figure out the words in the second column and write them.
Then draw lines to the same words in the first column.

1. watched •   • _ _ _ g _

2. bridge •   • _ _ _ _ _ _ _

3. clock •   • _ _ _ _ _ _

4. listen •   • _ _ _ _ _

5. large •   • _ _ i _ _ _

Lesson 40 is a test lesson. There is no worksheet.

LESSON 41

PART A

1. _____   6. _____
2. _____   7. _____
3. _____   8. _____
4. _____   9. _____
5. _____   10. _____

PART B

Graceful sailboats caught up with the rowboats.

_____

_____

PART C

1. _____   5. _____
2. _____   6. _____
3. _____   7. _____
4. _____   8. _____

PART D

1. _ o _ _ _   4. _ _ _ t _ _
2. _ _ t _ _   5. _ _ o u _ _ _
3. _ _ e _ _

41

Draw a line from each word to its clue.

1. meat   •
2. through   •
3. meet   •
4. would   •
5. wood   •

• We aren't _____ yet.

• This house is made of _____.

• How _____ you do this?

• The _____ is tough.

• When did I _____ you?

LESSON 42

PART A

1. _____

2. _____

PART B

1. _____   5. _____

2. _____   6. _____

3. _____   7. _____

4. _____   8. _____

PART C

__ __ace __ __l __ai__ __oa__ __ __augh__ __ __

____ ___ __ow_____.

_____

_____

PART D

1. _____   4. _____

2. _____   5. _____

3. _____   6. _____

43

Draw a line from each word to its clue.

1. write   •

2. meat   •

3. wood   •

4. through   •

  • We walked _____ the tunnel.

  • Can you _____ quickly?

  • That doll is made of _____.

  • a type of food

Cross out the misspelled words in these sentences.
Then write the words correctly above the crossed-out words.

Eat your meet with your forck.

Peeple wached from the roof.

LESSON 43

PART A

1. _____
2. _____

PART B

1. _____   5. _____
2. _____   6. _____
3. _____   7. _____
4. _____   8. _____

PART C

_ _ a c _ _ _ _ _   _ a i _ _ _ a _ _   _ a u _ _ _   _ _
_ _ _ _   _ _ _   _ _ w _ _ _ _ _.

_____

_____

PART D

1. _____   5. _____
2. _____   6. _____
3. _____   7. _____
4. _____   8. _____

45

Figure out the words in the second column and write them.
Then draw lines to the same words in the first column.

1. charge •
2. fringe •
3. ridge •
4. change •
5. badge •
6. nudge •

• _ a _ _ _
• _ h _ _ _ _
• _ _ d _ _
• _ i _ _ _
• _ _ _ n _ _
• _ r _ _ _ _

LESSON 44

PART A

1. press	3. boss	5. dress	7. mess	9. hiss
2. glass	4. bliss	6. class	8. loss	10. fuss

PART B

1. _____

2. _____

PART C

1. _____ 5. _____

2. _____ 6. _____

3. _____ 7. _____

4. _____ 8. _____

PART D

_ _ _ C _ _ _ _ _   _ _ i _ _ _ _ _   _ _ U _ _ _   _ _

_ _ _   _ _ _   _ _ _ _ _ _ _ .

_____

_____

47

These words are in the puzzle.
Circle 7 or more of the words.

b	b	c	b	b	m	f
h	p	o	r	t	e	i
a	r	u	u	a	s	l
p	e	n	s	n	s	l
p	s	t	h	e	d	h
y	s	s	p	e	l	l
c	w	o	n	d	e	r

brush   port   crash

press   happy   need

bound   wonder   spell

fill   mess   count

Lesson 45 is a test lesson. There is no worksheet.

48

LESSON 46

How _____ you _____ this report?

PART B

glass	race
fuss	voice
press	fence
bliss	nice
boss	place
dress	choice

PART C

1. _____

2. _____

PART D

1. o _ _ _ _ _

2. _ _ _ _ u _ _

3. _ _ _ i _ _ _

4. _ u _ _ _ _ _ _

5. _ _ _ _ e

6. _ _ a _

49

Write each of these words in a box.

brush   choice   happy   join   sell   brown   enough   huge

fill   change   found   fence   crash   dress   race   think

LESSON 47

PART A

1. _____

2. _____

PART B

1. _____ 5. _____

2. _____ 6. _____

3. _____ 7. _____

4. _____ 8. _____

PART C

Eight children left school together.

_____

_____

PART D

1. _ _ _ o _ 4. _ _ i _ _ _

2. _ _ _ _ l _ 5. _ _ _ _ _ _

3. _ _ _ p _ 6. _ _ _ t _ _

PART E

Draw a line from each word to its clue.

1. through •   • I _____ like some sleep.

2. write •   • Let's _____ at the park.

3. would •   • They marched _____ town.

4. meet •   • We want _____ and potatoes.

5. their •   • They own _____ home.

6. meat •   • with a pencil

LESSON 48

PART A

1. _____

2. _____

3. _____

4. _____

PART B

1. _____

2. _____

PART C

1. _____

2. _____

3. _____

4. _____

5. _____

6. _____

7. _____

8. _____

PART D

E i _ _ _   _ _ i _ re_   _ _ _ _   _ch_ _ _

_ o _ e _ _ _ _ .

_____

_____

rowboats	building	caught	people	friends
graceful	wonder	bridge	voice	listen
together	through	light	watched	thought
should	sailboats	tough	pledge	believe

PART **F**

Figure out the words in the second column and write them. Then draw lines to the same words in the first column.

1. motor •   • _ _ _ _ l _
2. should •   • _ _ _ _ d
3. happy •   • _ _ _ _ _ _
4. friend •   • _ _ t _ _
5. grand •   • _ _ _ t _ _
6. little •   • _ _ _ _ _

LESSON **49**

PART **A**

1. _____   4. _____
2. _____   5. _____
3. _____   6. _____

PART **B**

1. _____
2. _____

PART **C**

1. _____   5. _____
2. _____   6. _____
3. _____   7. _____
4. _____   8. _____

PART **D**

E____ __i____ ____ __h___ ___e____.

_____
_____

54

1. <u>Change</u> into that <u>dress</u> and get on the <u>staje</u>.   _____

2. My <u>boss</u> gave me a <u>hewge</u> <u>wage</u>.   _____

3. The <u>roeboats</u> lost the <u>race</u> to the <u>sailboats</u>.   _____

Cross out the misspelled words in these sentences.
Then write the words correctly above the crossed-out words.

I thought they wood lissen.

They love thair home.

· ·

Lesson 50 is a test lesson. There is no worksheet.

LESSON 51

PART A

_ _ _ _   _ _ _ _ _ _   _ _ _   _ _ _ _ _

_ _ _ _ _ _ _ .

_____

_____

PART B

1. ring
2. wonder
3. rent
4. act
5. water
6. pack
7. fresh
8. listen

PART C

1. _____ ring
2. _____ ringing
3. _____ wondering
4. _____ wonder
5. _____ renting
6. _____ react
7. _____ watering
8. _____ repacking

PART D

1. _____
2. _____
3. _____
4. _____

PART E

These words are in the puzzle.
Circle 7 or more of the words.

worth	count	shoot
ask	kept	write
wonder	stop	stone
shape	need	made

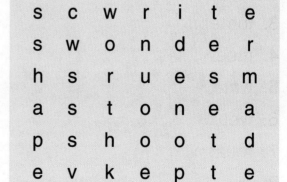

```
s  c  w  r  i  t  e
s  w  o  n  d  e  r
h  s  r  u  e  s  m
a  s  t  o  n  e  a
p  s  h  o  o  t  d
e  v  k  e  p  t  e
```

56

LESSON 52

PART A

1. _____

2. _____

PART B

1. rest   3. born   5. fresh   7. count   9. think

2. string   4. quiet   6. water   8. place   10. light

PART C

1. _____ resting   5. _____ quieting

2. _____ rest   6. _____ stringing

3. _____ string   7. _____ refreshing

4. _____ reborn   8. _____ watering

PART D

1. _____   3. _____

2. _____   4. _____

PART E

Draw a line from each word to its clue.

1. their   •   • When will you go _____?

2. right   •   • putting words on paper

3. through   •   • fuel for a fire

4. meet   •   • They found _____ money.

5. write   •   • a type of food

6. would   •   • not wrong

7. meat   •   • How _____ it feel to be a cat?

8. wood   •   • What time should we _____?

57

LESSON **53**

PART **A**

1. fresh	4. wonder	7. lock	10. place
2. rest	5. ring	8. pack	11. press
3. rent	6. happy	9. build	12. spend

PART **B**

1. _____ refresh
2. _____ resting
3. _____ rest
4. _____ rent

5. _____ refreshing
6. _____ wondering
7. _____ ringing
8. _____ ring

PART **C**

1. _____
2. _____
3. _____
4. _____

5. _____
6. _____
7. _____
8. _____

PART **D**

1. _____
2. _____

3. _____
4. _____

PART **E**

1. _____ + _____ = building
2. _____ + _____ = replace
3. _____ + _____ = pressing
4. _____ + _____ + _____ = unpacking
5. _____ + _____ = spending

58

PART F

1. Tim's <u>scool</u> is a <u>nice</u> <u>place</u>.   _____

2. The <u>moter</u> <u>left</u> black drops on their <u>grass</u>.   _____

3. <u>Eight</u> <u>children</u> ate <u>togethir</u>.   _____

4. I <u>could</u> hear a <u>trase</u> of fear in her <u>voice</u>.   _____

PART G

Cross out the misspelled words in these sentences.
Then write the words correctly above the crossed-out words.

Eite children left skool togather.

I beleve she is throogh.

LESSON 54

PART A

1. _____ fun
2. _____ unborn
3. _____ fresh

4. _____ refreshing
5. _____ rebuilding
6. _____ unhappy

PART B

1. _____

2. _____

PART C

1. _____
2. _____
3. _____

4. _____
5. _____
6. _____

PART D

Fill in the blanks to show the morphographs in each word.

1. _____ + _____ = coldest
2. _____ + _____ = wondering
3. _____ + _____ + _____ = unfolding
4. _____ + _____ = listening
5. _____ + _____ = greenest
6. _____ + _____ + _____ = rebuilding

60

1. This <u>place</u> looks <u>nice</u> <u>sinse</u> you painted it.   _____

2. Keep <u>track</u> of <u>whitch</u> <u>stage</u> you are in.   _____

3. Scott <u>didn't</u> <u>excape</u> the skunk's <u>spray</u>.   _____

4. "The <u>glass</u> is such a <u>mess</u>," she <u>sihged</u>.   _____

PART F

Figure out the words in the second column and write them.
Then draw lines to the same words in the first column.

1. glass	•	• <u>V</u> _ _ _ _
2. voice	•	• _ _ _ <u>C</u> _
3. change	•	• _ _ _ _ _ _
4. bridge	•	• _ _ _ _ <u>e</u>
5. thick	•	• _ _ <u>U</u> _ _
6. look	•	• _ _ _ <u>d</u> _ _
7. large	•	• _ _ _ <u>S</u> _
8. tough	•	• _ _ _ _

Lesson 55 is a test lesson. There is no worksheet.

LESSON 56

PART A

Draw a line from each morphograph to its meaning.

1. re •   • when you do something

2. ing •   • not

3. un •   • again

4. est •   • the most

PART B

1. _____   5. _____

2. _____   6. _____

3. _____   7. _____

4. _____   8. _____

PART C

-age   -ine   -oke

PART D

1. _____

2. _____

PART E

1. _____   4. _____

2. _____   5. _____

3. _____

62

PART F

1. There was little <u>space</u> left in <u>thier</u> <u>trunk</u>. _____

2. The <u>children</u> made a <u>choise</u> to go <u>left</u>. _____

3. Dad <u>wached</u> as the <u>truck</u> got <u>stuck</u> in the mud. _____

4. The <u>soot</u> made her <u>fase</u> and hands <u>black</u>. _____

PART G

Fill in the blanks to show the morphographs in each word.

1. _____ + _____ = refine

2. _____ + _____ = unsound

3. _____ + _____ = brownest

4. _____ + _____ = dressing

5. _____ + _____ + _____ = unkindest

6. _____ + _____ + _____ = unthinking

LESSON 57

PART A

-ake   -ide   -obe

PART B

Draw a line from each morphograph to its meaning.

1. re   •   • when you do something

2. ing   •   • without

3. un   •   • again

4. est   •   • the most

5. less   •   • not

PART C

1. _ a _ _

2. _ _ i _ _

3. _ o r _ _

4. _ _ _ _

5. _ _ _ _ e _

6. _ _ _ u _ _

PART D

1. _____   4. _____

2. _____   5. _____

3. _____   6. _____

PART E

Fill in the blanks to show the morphographs in each word.

1. _____ + _____ = friendless

2. _____ + _____ + _____ = unthinking

3. _____ + _____ + _____ = unkindest

4. _____ + _____ = worthless

5. _____ + _____ = rewrite

6. _____ + _____ = lightest

64

LESSON **58**

PART A

1. _____   5. _____
2. _____   6. _____
3. _____   7. _____
4. _____   8. _____

PART B

1. _____
2. _____

PART C

1. _____   4. _____
2. _____   5. _____
3. _____   6. _____

PART D

could	luck	real	book	want
reach	room	skill	listen	fight
these	those	spend	above	which
graceful	try	need	trick	trust
pledge	count	sold	change	tough

65

Draw a line from each morphograph to its meaning.

1. mis •		• not
2. less •		• again
3. est •		• wrong
4. un •		• when you do something
5. re •		• the most
6. ing •		• without

LESSON 59

PART A

equal   serve   human   great

PART B

The author wrote several different stories.

_____

_____

PART C

Fill in the blanks to show the morphographs in each word.

1. _____ + _____ + _____ = misspelling

2. _____ + _____ = unhappy

3. _____ + _____ + _____ = repacking

4. _____ + _____ = quietest

5. _____ + _____ = mistake

PART D

Draw a line from each word to its clue.

1. there •   • I would like to _____ a story.

2. right •   • They love _____ children.

3. meat •   • I _____ not touch that.

4. would •   • get together

5. through •   • We found them over _____.

6. their •   • This is not wrong. It's _____.

7. write •   • The ball went _____ the window.

8. meet •   • The _____ is tough.

• •

Lesson 60 is a test lesson. There is no worksheet.

67

LESSON 61

PART A

1. _____   5. _____

2. _____   6. _____

3. _____   7. _____

4. _____   8. _____

PART B

___ _u___o_ w___ ___e_a_
_____ere__ ____ie_.

_____

_____

PART C

Draw a line from each morphograph to its meaning.

1. un   •   • the most

2. mis   •   • again

3. re   •   • without

4. ing   •   • not

5. est   •   • when you do something

6. less •   • wrong

68

These words are in the puzzle.
Circle 7 or more of the words.

human	city	most
rest	made	author
done	above	serve
cube	great	ends

```
s  e  r  v  e  h
h  a  r  r  n  u
c  u  b  e  d  m
i  t  m  o  s  t
t  h  a  a  v  t
y  o  d  o  n  e
g  r  e  a  t  t
```

LESSON 62

PART A

1. _____   4. _____
2. _____   5. _____
3. _____   6. _____

PART B

_ _ _   _ u _ _ o   w _ _ _ _   _ _ _ _ _ a _
_ _ _ _ _ e _ e _ _   _ _ _ _ i _ .

_____

_____

PART C

1. _____

_____

2. _____

_____

PART D

Figure out the words in the second column and write them.
Then draw lines to the same words in the first column.

1. here   •   • _ _ o _ _
2. there •   • _ _ _ _
3. where •   • _ _ _ s _
4. these •   • _ l _ _ _
5. those •   • _ _ _ _ _
6. close •   • w _ _ _ _

Draw a line from each morphograph to its meaning.

1. mis •   • without

2. less •   • again

3. un •   • the most

4. est •   • wrong

5. ing •   • not

6. re •   • when you do something

1. You can <u>count</u> on <u>fresch</u>, <u>green</u> peppers.   _____

2. The fish <u>could</u> <u>act</u> lively in the <u>cooldest</u> water.   _____

3. I was <u>happy</u> <u>lissening</u> to the <u>birds</u>.   _____

LESSON 63

PART A

charm   cheap   child   choke   chalk   chill

PART B

1. _____   5. _____
2. _____   6. _____
3. _____   7. _____
4. _____   8. _____

PART C

_ _ _   _u_ _ _ _   w_ _ _ _   _ _ _ _ _a_

_ _ _ _ _ _ _e_ _   _ _ _ _ _i_ _.

_____

_____

PART D

value   break   length   strength

PART E

Draw a line from each morphograph to its meaning.

1. un   •   • wrong

2. less •   • not

3. re   •   • when you do something

4. est   •   • again

5. ing   •   • without

6. mis   •   • the most

Fill in the blanks to show the morphographs in each word.

1. _____ + _____ + _____ = misspelling
2. _____ + _____ = unequal
3. _____ + _____ = greatest
4. _____ + _____ = pointless
5. _____ + _____ = rewrite
6. _____ + _____ = charming

PART **G**

1. <u>Thank</u> you for un<u>pakking</u> the <u>rest</u> of the stuff. _____
2. That <u>thick</u> <u>string</u> came <u>undun</u>. _____
3. <u>Peopel</u> who cannot see well need <u>large</u> <u>print</u>. _____
4. I had to <u>spend</u> a lot to <u>replase</u> the <u>ring</u>. _____

LESSON 64

PART A

b u h o t e i n c
a f r u s g i m o

PART B

1. _____   5. _____
2. _____   6. _____
3. _____   7. _____
4. _____   8. _____

PART C

1. _____
2. _____

PART D

1. _____   4. _____
2. _____   5. _____
3. _____   6. _____

PART E

Cross out the misspelled words in these sentences.
Then write the words correctly above the crossed-out words.

The freinds did not have equil strength.

My dog acts like a humen.

I thowght that I wanted to werk hard.

··
Lesson 65 is a test lesson. There is no worksheet.

74

© SRA/McGraw-Hill. All rights reserved.

LESSON 66

PART A

Make a small **v** above every vowel letter.
Make a small **c** above every consonant letter.

n   e   c   j   k   o   v   d   l

p   a   r   f   u   e   i   o   t

PART B

1. _____   5. _____
2. _____   6. _____
3. _____   7. _____
4. _____   8. _____

PART C

1. _____
2. _____

PART D

1. _____   4. _____
2. _____   5. _____
3. _____   6. _____

75

Draw a line from each word to its clue.

1. feat •
2. there •
3. write •
4. meat •
5. their •
6. right •
7. would •
8. through •

• they own it
• Why did you _____ that note?
• an act of great skill
• We put the thread _____ the needle.
• Where _____ they put this?
• We found the toys over _____.
• correct
• I like cold _____ and gravy.

LESSON 67

PART A

-atch   -etch   -itch   -otch

PART B

1. _____

2. _____

PART C

1. _ _ _ _ _ _   3. _ _ _ _ _ _   5. _ _   _ _ _ _

2. _ _ _ _ _   4. _ _ _ _ _ _   6. _ _ _ _ _

PART D

Write each of these words in a box.

size	wrote	repay	cure
helpless	fire	there	large
want	strength	charming	eight
workable	judge	school	these

Make a small **v** above every vowel letter.
Make a small **c** above every consonant letter.

a   c   i   m   s   u   d   o   p

v   e   o   u   n   t   z   r   k

LESSON 68

© SRA/McGraw-Hill. All rights reserved.

PART A

-atch   -etch   -itch   -otch

PART B

1. _____   4. _____

2. _____   5. _____

3. _____   6. _____

PART C

1. _____

2. _____

PART D

Fill in the blanks to show the morphographs in each word.

1. _____ + _____ = report

2. _____ + _____ = portable

3. _____ + _____ + _____ = unworkable

4. _____ + _____ = roughness

5. _____ + _____ + _____ = thoughtlessness

6. _____ + _____ + _____ = misspelling

7. _____ + _____ + _____ = unbreakable

PART E

Make a small **v** above every vowel letter.
Make a small **c** above every consonant letter.

u   b   n   i   o   k   l

a   e   g   t   i   h   a

79

LESSON 69

PART A

1. <u>catch</u>   4. <u>match</u>

2. <u>ditch</u>   5. stre<u>tch</u>

3. <u>n</u>otch   6. s<u>titch</u>

PART B

Write the word for each meaning.

word	meaning
1. _____	not sure
2. _____	without need
3. _____	build again
4. _____	that which is quiet
5. _____	judge wrong
6. _____	able to be washed

PART C

1. _____	4. _____
2. _____	5. _____
3. _____	6. _____

PART D

Make a small **v** above every vowel letter.
Make a small **c** above every consonant letter.

b   r   e   n   o   p   z

i   a   j   u   k   i   e

80

Draw a line from each morphograph to its meaning.

1. able •   •   in the past

2. mis •   •   able to be

3. ed •   •   without

4. re •   •   that which is

5. less •   •   not

6. ing •   •   wrong

7. ness •   •   when you do something

8. un •   •   again

PART **F**

1. The <u>auther</u> had to <u>rewrite</u> his stories <u>several</u>   _____
   times.

2. Be <u>safe</u> when you <u>driv</u> to the <u>lake</u>.   _____

3. The <u>smoke</u> seemed to put the <u>snake</u> under   _____
   a <u>spel</u>.

• •

Lesson 70 is a test lesson. There is no worksheet.

LESSON 71

PART A

civil   search   touch   view

PART B

1. _____

2. _____

3. _____

4. _____

5. _____

6. _____

PART C

1. _____

2. _____

3. _____

4. _____

5. _____

6. _____

PART D

Write the word for each meaning.

word	meaning
1. _____	help in the past
2. _____	that which is dark
3. _____	able to work
4. _____	not happy
5. _____	spell wrong
6. _____	without rest

82

Fill in the blanks to show the morphographs in each word.

1. _____ + _____ + _____ = unkindest
2. _____ + _____ + _____ = repacked
3. _____ + _____ + _____ = pointlessness
4. _____ + _____ = remark
5. _____ + _____ = roughness
6. _____ + _____ + _____ = mismatched
7. _____ + _____ = brushing
8. _____ + _____ + _____ = unsoundness

PART **F**

1. A <u>child</u> can easily <u>break</u> <u>chock</u>.   _____

2. Our <u>leeder</u> did not <u>blame</u> anyone for the <u>mistake</u>.   _____

3. I <u>value</u> her <u>strenth</u> and <u>charm</u>.   _____

4. The grapes on the <u>vine</u> are too <u>ripe</u> to be <u>werth</u> much.   _____

LESSON 72

PART A

1. _____   4. _____

2. _____   5. _____

3. _____   6. _____

PART B

1. _____

2. _____

PART C

1. _ _ _ _ n _   4. _ o u c _

2. _ i e _   5. _ e a _ _ _

3. _ _ _ i _   6. _ e _ _ _

PART D

1. like + able   = _____

2. write + ing   = _____

3. smoke + ing = _____

4. green + est = _____

5. pure + est   = _____

6. use + able   = _____

7. shine + ing = _____

8. dark + ness = _____

Draw a line from each word to its clue.

1. feet •   • Put your things over _____ .

2. witch •   • not left

3. there •   • Let's _____ before school.

4. feat •   • The fire jumper landed on her _____ .

5. right •   • This _____ is very hard.

6. their •   • doing something great

7. wood •   • a make-believe person

8. meet •   • They like _____ new game.

LESSON 73

PART A

1. _____   4. _____
2. _____   5. _____
3. _____   6. _____

PART B

1. _____
2. _____

PART C

1. fine + est   = _____
2. cure + able   = _____
3. ripe + ness   = _____
4. worth + less   = _____
5. hope + less   = _____
6. stage + ing   = _____
7. judge + ed   = _____
8. shame + less   = _____

Write each of these words in a box.

through	value	touch	sack
grounded	replace	search	view
change	mistake	large	since
break	bridge	length	worth

PART **E**

Write the word for each meaning.

	word	**meaning**
1.	_____	start in the past
2.	_____	without worth
3.	_____	the most fresh
4.	_____	shrunk before
5.	_____	without speech
6.	_____	that which is cold

LESSON 74

PART A

1. _____   4. _____

2. _____   5. _____

3. _____   6. _____

PART B

1. _____

2. _____

PART C

1. _____   5. _____

2. _____   6. _____

3. _____   7. _____

4. _____   8. _____

PART D

Add these morphographs together.
Some of the words follow the rule about dropping an **e.**

1. large + est   = _____

2. change + less = _____

3. race + ing   = _____

4. fine + ness   = _____

5. work + able   = _____

6. hire + ed   = _____

7. wide + est   = _____

8. shape + ing   = _____

88

PART E

1. _____   4. _____

2. _____   5. _____

3. _____   6. _____

PART F

Draw a line from each morphograph to its meaning.

1. ed   •   •   before

2. able   •   •   in the past

3. ness   •   •   wrong

4. pre   •   •   that which is

5. re   •   •   again

6. mis   •   •   able to be

PART G

1. We cannot lay this <u>pipe</u> on such <u>uneven</u>   _____
   <u>grownd</u>.

2. <u>Slice</u> that into <u>equel</u> <u>lengths</u>.   _____

3. <u>Reech</u> under it with the <u>side</u> of the <u>rake</u>. _____

4. Only <u>hier</u> the <u>kindest</u> <u>people</u> for the job. _____

• •

Lesson 75 is a test lesson. There is no worksheet.

89

LESSON 76

PART A

1. There is a <u>larje</u> house over there. Ⓡ Ⓦ
2. Don't walk over that <u>brige</u>. Ⓡ Ⓦ
3. I found a <u>worthless</u> coin. Ⓡ Ⓦ
4. Were you <u>lissening</u> to me? Ⓡ Ⓦ
5. We <u>should</u> know that answer. Ⓡ Ⓦ
6. Those people like <u>there</u> home. Ⓡ Ⓦ

PART B

1. k _ _ w
2. _ _ _ g h _
3. _ _ u _ _

4. _ _ r _ _ _
5. _ _ _ e _
6. _ _ _ s _ _ _ _

PART C

1. _____ + _____ = _____
2. _____ + _____ = _____
3. _____ + _____ = _____
4. _____ + _____ = _____
5. _____ + _____ = _____
6. _____ + _____ = _____

PART D

Wash the clothes with the new soap.

_____

_____

90

Fill in the blanks to show the morphographs in each word.

1. _____ + _____ = boundless

2. _____ + _____ + _____ = unbreakable

3. _____ + _____ + _____ = helplessness

4. _____ + _____ + _____ = misspelling

5. _____ + _____ + _____ = refillable

6. _____ + _____ = building

7. _____ + _____ = colder

8. _____ + _____ + _____ + _____ = unrefreshing

LESSON 77

PART A

Fill in the circle marked **R** if the underlined word is spelled right.
Fill in the circle marked **W** if the underlined word is spelled wrong.

1. They found the boys <u>togather</u>. Ⓡ Ⓦ
2. Can you <u>teach</u> me that trick? Ⓡ Ⓦ
3. I will see you after <u>skool</u>. Ⓡ Ⓦ
4. We have <u>sevral</u> different coins. Ⓡ Ⓦ
5. That answer isn't <u>write</u>. Ⓡ Ⓦ
6. Did you <u>misspell</u> that word? Ⓡ Ⓦ

PART B

1. _____ + _____ = _____
2. _____ + _____ = _____
3. _____ + _____ = _____
4. _____ + _____ = _____
5. _____ + _____ = _____
6. _____ + _____ = _____

PART C

_a_ _ ___ _____e s ____
___ _ew _oa_.

_____

_____

92

1. _____   5. _____
2. _____   6. _____
3. _____   7. _____
4. _____   8. _____

PART E

Draw a line from each morphograph to its meaning.

1. ly   •   •   in the past
2. ness   •   •   not
3. mis   •   •   that which is
4. un   •   •   how something is
5. pre   •   •   more, one who
6. er   •   •   without
7. less   •   •   wrong
8. ed   •   •   before

PART F

1. Nikki <u>thought</u> the <u>glass</u> was <u>unbrakeable</u>.   _____
2. If you <u>strech</u> it too far, it <u>could</u> <u>break</u>.   _____
3. Don't <u>make</u> a <u>mistake</u> and <u>mispell</u> this word.   _____

93

PART A

1. _____ + _____ = _____
2. _____ + _____ = _____
3. _____ + _____ = _____
4. _____ + _____ = _____
5. _____ + _____ = _____
6. _____ + _____ = _____

PART B

_ a _ _   _ _ _   _ _ _ _ _ e _   _ _ _ _

_ _ _   _ w _   _ _ a _.

_____

_____

PART C

1. _____   4. _____

2. _____   5. _____

3. _____   6. _____

PART D

Fill in the circle marked **R** if the underlined word is spelled right.
Fill in the circle marked **W** if the underlined word is spelled wrong.

1. Those <u>peeple</u> are very nice.   Ⓡ   Ⓦ
2. How many <u>children</u> are here?   Ⓡ   Ⓦ
3. They can't find <u>there</u> sister.   Ⓡ   Ⓦ
4. This balloon won't <u>strech</u> any further.   Ⓡ   Ⓦ
5. I <u>would</u> like to look for gold.   Ⓡ   Ⓦ

94

LESSON 79

1. _____ + _____ = tracing
2. _____ + _____ = careless
3. _____ + _____ = faced
4. _____ + _____ = usable
5. _____ + _____ = likely
6. _____ + _____ = sizable

PART B

_ _ _ _   _ _ _   _ _ _ _ _ _   _ _ _ _

_ _ _   _ _ _   _ _ _ _.

_____

_____

PART C

1. _____
2. _____
3. _____
4. _____

5. _____
6. _____
7. _____
8. _____

Add these morphographs together.
Some of the words follow the rule about dropping an **e.**

1. re + place + ed = _____
2. hope + less + ly = _____
3. re + serve + ed = _____
4. pre + view + ed = _____
5. un + use + able = _____
6. un + equal + ly = _____

PART **E**

These words are in the puzzle.
Circle 7 or more of the words.

counting	point	joined
jet	smart	found
sprint	neat	lost
sigh	bring	new

p	j	f	l	c	s	m
s	o	e	o	o	l	t
m	i	i	t	u	s	t
a	n	g	n	n	n	t
r	e	e	h	t	e	d
t	d	s	w	i	a	d
s	p	r	i	n	t	g
b	r	i	n	g	g	d

PART **F**

1. I was <u>hired</u> to <u>teech</u> <u>preschool</u>. _____
2. She <u>reveiwed</u> her <u>speech</u> near the <u>stage</u>. _____
3. The <u>charming</u> <u>home</u> had a nice <u>veiw</u>. _____

Lesson 80 is a test lesson. There is no worksheet.

96

LESSON 81

PART A

1. _____

2. _____

PART B

1. _____ + _____ = caring

2. _____ + _____ = shameless

3. _____ + _____ = misspell

4. _____ + _____ = sizable

5. _____ + _____ + _____ = hopelessly

6. _____ + _____ = purest

7. _____ + _____ + _____ = reviewed

8. _____ + _____ = racing

PART C

1. _____   5. _____

2. _____   6. _____

3. _____   7. _____

4. _____   8. _____

Add these morphographs together.
Some of the words follow the rule about dropping an **e.**

1. hire + ed   = _____

2. shape + ing   = _____

3. like + ness   = _____

4. point + less   = _____

5. large + ly   = _____

6. like + able   = _____

7. break + able   = _____

8. stage + ing   = _____

Figure out the words in the second column and write them.
Then draw lines to the same words in the first column.

1. shame   •   • _ _ n _ _ h

2. clothes •   • _ _ _ _ _ _ _

3. twice   •   • _ e _ _ _ _

4. length   •   • _ _ _ t _ _ _

5. stretch •   • _ _ _ m _

6. search   •   • _ _ i _ _

7. strength •   • _ _ _ _ _

8. value   •   • _ _ _ _ _ _ _

98

LESSON 82

PART A

1. _____

2. _____

PART B

1. _____   4. _____

2. _____   5. _____

3. _____   6. _____

PART C

Write each word in a box.

harmlessly   valuable   fright   brightness

unreachable   sketching   every   slightest

preserve   stretcher   civil   nightly

fighter   preshrunk   catcher   length

Fill in the blanks to show the morphographs in each word.

1. _____ + _____ + _____ = preserving
2. _____ + _____ + _____ = rehiring
3. _____ + _____ = blameless
4. _____ + _____ + _____ = uselessness
5. _____ + _____ + _____ = unlikely
6. _____ + _____ = listening
7. _____ + _____ + _____ = resorted
8. _____ + _____ = bluest

Draw a line from each word to its clue.

1. witch •   • I don't know _____ I like better.
2. feat •   • Put these things _____, please.
3. which •   • get together
4. wood •   • The _____ is dressed in black.
5. meet •   • Will you _____ me a letter?
6. write •   • not wrong
7. there •   • something great
8. right •   • We burn _____ in our stove.

100

LESSON 83

bite   kite   quite   white   spite

PART B

1. _____

2. _____

PART C

1. _____   4. _____

2. _____   5. _____

3. _____   6. _____

PART D

Fill in the blanks to show the morphographs in each word.

1. _____ + _____ = fineness

2. _____ + _____ = sizable

3. _____ + _____ = biting

4. _____ + _____ + _____ = replaced

5. _____ + _____ + _____ = misjudged

6. _____ + _____ = namely

7. _____ + _____ = shameless

8. _____ + _____ = fired

Draw a line from each word to its clue.

1. ly   •   • not
2. er   •   • in the past
3. pre   •   • when you do something
4. ed   •   • more, one who
5. able   •   • able to be
6. ness   •   • wrong
7. mis   •   • how something is
8. less   •   • the most
9. est   •   • again
10. un   •   • before
11. ing   •   • that which is
12. re   •   • without

1. After Bill's <u>remarck</u>, the <u>child</u> was <u>speechless</u>.   _____
2. <u>Wash</u> it <u>twice</u> with this <u>sope</u>.   _____
3. That <u>feat</u> <u>took</u> <u>scill</u>.   _____

102

LESSON **84**

PART **A**

1. _____   6. _____

2. _____   7. _____

3. _____   8. _____

4. _____   9. _____

5. _____   10. _____

PART **B**

1. C _ _ _   4. _ _ i _ _ _

2. _ _ _ _   5. _ _ l _

3. _ _ w _   6. _ _ _ s _

PART **C**

Add these morphographs together.
Some of the words follow the rule about dropping an **e**.

1. race + ing   = _____

2. re + name + ing   = _____

3. white + est   = _____

4. probe + ing   = _____

5. pure + ness   = _____

6. wide + ly   = _____

7. bake + er   = _____

8. life + less   = _____

103

Write the word for each meaning.

word	meaning
1. _____	build again
2. _____	judge wrong
3. _____	able to work
4. _____	the most kind
5. _____	that which is good
6. _____	without a home
7. _____	one who teaches
8. _____	not sold

PART E

1. We <u>searched</u> <u>throogh</u> the <u>darkness</u>.   _____

2. They <u>needlesly</u> <u>fired</u> the <u>reviewer.</u>   _____

• •

Lesson 85 is a test lesson. There is no worksheet.

LESSON 86

PART A

1. pack	3. big	5. plan	7. stop	9. clap
2. flat	4. wonder	6. charm	8. civil	10. fit

PART B

1. _____

2. _____

PART C

able	cure	work	ing	un	like

1. _____   5. _____

2. _____   6. _____

3. _____   7. _____

4. _____   8. _____

PART D

Fill in the blanks to show the morphographs in each word.

1. _____ + _____ + _____ = previewed

2. _____ + _____ + _____ = unequally

3. _____ + _____ = whitest

4. _____ + _____ + _____ = unusable

5. _____ + _____ + _____ = researching

6. _____ + _____ + _____ = thoughtlessly

7. _____ + _____ = valuable

8. _____ + _____ = civilly

105

Cross out the misspelled words in these sentences.
Then write the words correctly above the crossed-out words.

My friend rote a towching story.

That illness is not cureable.

PART F

1. I love the <u>pureness</u> and <u>briteness</u> of <u>white</u>
   snow.   _____

2. The <u>kite</u> became <u>lifeless</u> as it <u>quitly</u> sank to   _____
   the ground.

3. Our <u>driving</u> <u>time</u> was <u>twise</u> as long as yours.   _____

106

LESSON 87

PART A

1. _ _ _ e _
2. _ _ _ _ _
3. _ _ _ _ n g _ _

4. _ _ _ _ _ _ _
5. _ _ _ u _ _ _
6. _ _ _ _ _ _ _

PART B

1. flop
2. human
3. star
4. kite
5. drag

6. list
7. run
8. snap
9. plan
10. water

PART C

like	able	ing	stretch	note	ed	use

1. _____
2. _____
3. _____
4. _____
5. _____
6. _____

7. _____
8. _____
9. _____
10. _____
11. _____

Draw a line from each morphograph to its meaning.

1. mis   •   • in the past

2. ness   •   • not

3. less   •   • that which is

4. able   •   • one who, more

5. ed   •   • wrong

6. est   •   • before

7. pre   •   • without

8. un   •   • how something is

9. re   •   • when you do something

10. er   •   • able to be

11. ing   •   • the most

12. ly   •   • again

1. My <u>new</u> car was even <u>cheeper</u> than I <u>thought</u>.   _____

2. She <u>parked</u> <u>there</u> <u>nitely</u>.   _____

3. Flowers were <u>nicely</u> <u>placed</u> along the <u>fense</u>.   _____

LESSON 88

PART A

That person often paints pictures.

_____

_____

PART B

1. _____   4. _____

2. _____   5. _____

3. _____   6. _____

PART C

Circle each short word that ends **cvc**.
Remember: Short words have four letters or less.

1. plan   3. arm   5. step   7. trip

2. rest   4. big   6. brother   8. drop

PART D

1. _____

2. _____

Add these morphographs together.
Some of the words follow the rule about dropping an **e**.

1. value + able = _____

2. like + ing = _____

3. fine + er = _____

4. fine + ness = _____

5. fine + ly = _____

6. time + less = _____

7. use + less = _____

8. use + ing = _____

9. trace + ing = _____

10. safe + ly = _____

11. wide + ness = _____

12. wide + ly = _____

13. wide + est = _____

14. serve + ing = _____

15. love + able = _____

PART F

1. I <u>know</u> the water is <u>likly</u> to be <u>rougher</u> this time. _____

2. Tom <u>hoped</u> the <u>search</u> would be <u>valueable</u>. _____

3. It is never <u>useless</u> to <u>surch</u> for a <u>cure</u>. _____

110

LESSON 89

PART A

1. _____   5. _____
2. _____   6. _____
3. _____   7. _____
4. _____   8. _____

PART B

_____ _____o_ __te_ _ai___
__ctu_e_.

_____

_____

PART C

1. _ i _ _ _   3. _ _ _ l _   5. _ _ _ _ _
2. _ _ _ a _   4. _ _ _ _

PART D

1. _____ + _____ = _____
2. _____ + _____ = _____
3. _____ + _____ = _____
4. _____ + _____ = _____
5. _____ + _____ = _____
6. _____ + _____ = _____

111

PART E

Circle each short word that ends **cvc**.
Remember: Short words have four letters or less.

1. motor   3. time   5. spot   7. fill

2. mad   4. smell   6. run   8. drop

PART F

Fill in the blanks to show the morphographs in each word.

1. _____ + _____ + _____ = helplessness

2. _____ + _____ = quietly

3. _____ + _____ = formless

4. _____ + _____ = friendly

5. _____ + _____ = stretcher

6. _____ + _____ + _____ = unpacked

7. _____ + _____ = timely

8. _____ + _____ = serving

9. _____ + _____ = staging

10. _____ + _____ = ripeness

Lesson 90 is a test lesson. There is no worksheet.

LESSON 91

© SRA/McGraw-Hill. All rights reserved.

PART A

1. shop + er = _____

2. help + er = _____

3. stop + ing = _____

4. run + ing = _____

5. form + ed = _____

6. ship + ed = _____

PART B

_ _ _ _   _ _ _ _ o _   _ _ t _ _   _ a _ _ _ _

_ _ _ t u _ _ _ .

_____

_____

PART C

Add these morphographs together.
Some of the words follow the rule about dropping an **e**.

1. slight + est   = _____

2. nice + est   = _____

3. care + ing   = _____

4. un + work + able   = _____

5. pre + serve + ing   = _____

6. de + serve + ed   = _____

113

Draw a line from each morphograph to its meaning.

1. de •   • how something is

2. ly •   • that which is

3. ness •   • in the past

4. pre •   • more, one who

5. re •   • down, away from

6. er •   • again

7. less •   • without

8. ed •   • before

These words are in the puzzle.
Circle 7 or more of the words.

speller	deal	city
hear	spend	rake
serve	care	press
grade	have	part

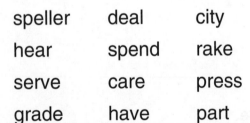

1. The <u>baker</u> took a <u>bite</u> of <u>wite</u> cake.   _____

2. <u>Pikking</u> ripe <u>bananas</u> is <u>pointless</u>.   _____

114

LESSON 92

PART A

Double when cvc + v

1. form + ing = _____
2. sad + er   = _____
3. swim + er = _____
4. help + ing = _____
5. mad + est = _____
6. run + er   = _____

PART B

_ _ _ _   _ _ _ _ _ _   _ _ _ _ _   _ _ _ _ _ _

_ _ _ _ _ _ _ _.

_____

_____

PART C

1. _____   5. _____
2. _____   6. _____
3. _____   7. _____
4. _____   8. _____

Fill in the blanks to show the morphographs in each word.

1. _____ + _____ + _____ = redefine

2. _____ + _____ + _____ = unequally

3. _____ + _____ = forceful

4. _____ + _____ + _____ = reserved

5. _____ + _____ = choicest

6. _____ + _____ + _____ + _____ = unrefined

7. _____ + _____ + _____ = misused

8. _____ + _____ = devalue

Write the word for each meaning.

word	meaning
1. _____	that which is thick
2. _____	stretch in the past
3. _____	the most fresh
4. _____	full of help
5. _____	shrunk before
6. _____	the most grand
7. _____	one who fights
8. _____	more white

116

LESSON 93

PART A

sign   fault   care   bare   carry

PART B

hope   slope   rope   scope   cope

PART C

1. _____

2. _____

PART D

Double when cvc + v

1. farm + er   = _____

2. swim + er   = _____

3. firm + est   = _____

4. sad + est   = _____

5. wash + ing = _____

6. snap + ing = _____

Make 11 real words from the morphographs in the box.

less	care	rest	ed	ful	ing	hope

1. _____   7. _____

2. _____   8. _____

3. _____   9. _____

4. _____   10. _____

5. _____   11. _____

6. _____

PART **F**

Draw a line from each morphograph to its meaning.

1. ful   •   •   before

2. de   •   •   more, one who

3. ly   •   •   down, away from

4. er   •   •   in the past

5. pre   •   •   that which is

6. ness   •   •   without

7. less   •   •   full of

8. ed   •   •   how something is

LESSON 94

PART A

1. _ _ _ _   4. _ _ u _ _
2. _ _ g _   5. _ _ _ r _
3. _ _ _ _   6. _ _ _ _ e

PART B

Double when cvc + v

1. stop + ing = _____
2. farm + er   = _____
3. plan + ed   = _____
4. sad + en   = _____
5. wash + ing = _____
6. run + er   = _____
7. form + ed   = _____
8. mad + est   = _____

PART C

Fill in the circle marked **R** if the underlined word is spelled right.
Fill in the circle marked **W** if the underlined word is spelled wrong.

1. Is that a <u>which</u> on that broom?   Ⓡ   Ⓦ
2. We like that <u>persen</u> very much.   Ⓡ   Ⓦ
3. They shared the money <u>equally</u>.   Ⓡ   Ⓦ
4. I was <u>hopeing</u> you would be there.   Ⓡ   Ⓦ
5. Is that ball made from <u>would</u> or rubber? Ⓡ   Ⓦ
6. He <u>misjuged</u> her strength.   Ⓡ   Ⓦ

Draw a line from each word to its clue.

1. tail •   • My _____ are too big for these shoes.

2. feat •   • I don't know _____ puppy to pick.

3. feet •   • correct

4. tale •   • That monkey has a long _____.

5. write •   • Those people lost _____ way.

6. which •   • How quickly can you _____?

7. their •   • something great

8. right •   • a story

PART **E**

1. My aunt <u>paints</u> <u>unbeleivable</u> <u>pictures</u>.   _____

2. That <u>persen</u> can tell a <u>tale</u> <u>unlike</u> any other.   _____

3. She <u>thoughtlessly</u> <u>noted</u> the person who was   _____
   <u>niser</u>.

••

Lesson 95 is a test lesson. There is no worksheet.

LESSON 96

PART A

1. _____

2. _____

PART B

1. _____   5. _____

2. _____   6. _____

3. _____   7. _____

4. _____

PART C

Double when cvc + v

1. stop + ing   = _____

2. shop + ed   = _____

3. farm + er   = _____

4. trip + ed   = _____

5. sad + est   = _____

6. wash + able = _____

7. snap + ed   = _____

8. plan + ing   = _____

1. face
   unnamed
   trase
   friendly

   _____

2. awthor
   freshness
   equal
   motor

   _____

3. spelling
   stretch
   author
   happey

   _____

4. change
   sirve
   trace
   reserve

   _____

5. blissful
   force
   preserve
   moter

   _____

6. page
   chandge
   stretcher
   match

   _____

PART E

Add these morphographs together.
Some of the words follow the rule about dropping an **e.**

1. civil + ly   = _____
2. un + change + ing   = _____
3. gold + en   = _____
4. de + fine + ed   = _____
5. pack + age + ing   = _____
6. de + code + ing   = _____
7. un + ripe + en + ed = _____
8. hope + ful + ly   = _____
9. de + light + ed   = _____
10. value + able   = _____

122

LESSON 97

PART A

world   wander   nerve   verb   herb

PART B

Circle the misspelled word in each group.
Then write it correctly on the line.

1. strength
   friendly
   pichure
   equally

   _____

2. juge
   preview
   listen
   nicely

   _____

3. nightly
   thaught
   touch
   spelling

   _____

4. mispell
   carry
   widely
   unpacked

   _____

5. stretch
   watch
   reatch
   switch

   _____

6. motor
   lightest
   preserve
   helplesness

   _____

PART C

Double when cvc + v

1. star + ing   = _____
2. talk + ed   = _____
3. hot + ly   = _____
4. plan + er   = _____
5. big + est   = _____
6. grand + ly   = _____
7. sad + ness = _____
8. win + er   = _____

PART **E**

1. en   •

2. ful   •

3. de   •

4. ly   •

5. pre   •

6. ness   •

7. er   •

8. re   •

9. less   •

10. ing   •

• more, one who

• down, away from

• that which is

• without

• make

• again

• full of

• when you do something

• how something is

• before

PART **F**

1. We will be <u>useing</u> only the <u>freshest</u> and <u>finest</u> beans.   _____

2. Meg <u>helped</u> <u>teach</u> the <u>speach</u> class.   _____

LESSON 98

time	er	help	smoke	less	ed	use

1. _____
2. _____
3. _____
4. _____
5. _____
6. _____

7. _____
8. _____
9. _____
10. _____
11. _____

PART B

1. _____
2. _____
3. _____
4. _____

5. _____
6. _____
7. _____
8. _____

PART C

Double when cvc + v

1. sad + ness = _____
2. drop + ing = _____
3. spot + ed = _____
4. hot + ly = _____
5. win + er = _____
6. star + less = _____

125

Add these morphographs together.
Remember to use your spelling rules.

1. sign + al   = _____
2. fault + less   = _____
3. person + able   = _____
4. globe + al   = _____
5. use + age   = _____
6. weak + en   = _____
7. de + sign   = _____
8. re + coil + ed   = _____
9. de + serve + ing   = _____
10. un + equal + ly   = _____

PART **E**

1. She packed <u>quite</u> a <u>sizable</u> <u>lunsh</u>.   _____
2. The <u>clothes</u> gave them a <u>remarckable</u> <u>clue</u>.   _____
3. <u>People</u> will be <u>useing</u> a <u>switch</u> to turn on the   _____
   lights.

126

LESSON 99

PART A

1. _____   5. _____
2. _____   6. _____
3. _____   7. _____
4. _____   8. _____

PART B

1. _____
2. _____

PART C

Double when cvc + v

1. big + er   = _____
2. shop + er   = _____
3. fit + ness   = _____
4. plan + ed   = _____
5. swim + er   = _____
6. mad + ness   = _____

Circle the misspelled word in each group.
Then write it correctly in the blank.

1. cownt
   hoping
   people
   shine

   _____

2. touching
   widest
   carrey
   beetle

   _____

3. helpful
   search
   greatest
   misplase

   _____

4. patch
   older
   holdding
   cheaper

   _____

5. winner
   watering
   valueing
   unkindness

   _____

6. strenght
   stretcher
   toughness
   together

   _____

1. She <u>deserved</u> to <u>lengthen</u> her <u>restfull</u> trip.   _____

2. Be <u>careful</u> when you <u>carrie</u> that <u>rope</u>.   _____

3. <u>Would</u> it be <u>helpful</u> to <u>frechen</u> up?   _____

Lesson 100 is a test lesson. There is no worksheet.

128

LESSON 101

© SRA/McGraw-Hill. All rights reserved.

PART A

1. happy
2. boy
3. you
4. yellow

5. berry
6. sturdy
7. play

PART B

1. _____ + _____ = _____
2. _____ + _____ = _____
3. _____ + _____ = _____
4. _____ + _____ = _____
5. _____ + _____ = _____
6. _____ + _____ = _____

PART C

1. _____
2. _____
3. _____
4. _____
5. _____
6. _____
7. _____

8. _____
9. _____
10. _____
11. _____
12. _____
13. _____
14. _____

1. _____ + _____ = swimmer
2. _____ + _____ = running
3. _____ + _____ = barely
4. _____ + _____ = driving
5. _____ + _____ = equally
6. _____ + _____ = maddest

PART **E**

Add these morphographs together.

1. large + ly   = _____
2. take + en   = _____
3. dose + age   = _____
4. globe + al   = _____
5. change + ing   = _____
6. pack + age + ing = _____

PART **F**

1. Our <u>nightly</u> <u>searching</u> went on <u>hoplessly</u>.   _____

2. The <u>swimming</u> pool near us has the <u>pureest</u> <u>water</u>.   _____

3. The <u>persen</u> felt <u>helpless</u> to change the <u>sadness</u> in her life.   _____

LESSON 102

PART A

1. _____ + _____ = _____
2. _____ + _____ = _____
3. _____ + _____ = _____
4. _____ + _____ = _____
5. _____ + _____ = _____
6. _____ + _____ = _____

PART B

1. _____
2. _____

PART C

Fill in the blanks to show the morphographs in each word.

1. _____ + _____ = trapped
2. _____ + _____ = brownish
3. _____ + _____ = yardage
4. _____ + _____ = dripping
5. _____ + _____ = slipped
6. _____ + _____ = rental
7. _____ + _____ + _____ = delightful
8. _____ + _____ = design
9. _____ + _____ = signal
10. _____ + _____ + _____ = unsnapped

Make 10 real words from the morphographs in the box.

like	wide	en	ing	ness	length	take	ly

1. _____   6. _____
2. _____   7. _____
3. _____   8. _____
4. _____   9. _____
5. _____   10. _____

1. I am <u>hopeing</u> that he hasn't <u>misjudged</u> the car's <u>power</u>.   _____

2. The <u>farmers</u> <u>planted</u> <u>valueable</u> crops.   _____

3. We were pleased with the <u>nicly</u> <u>packaged</u> <u>presents</u>.   _____

132

LESSON 103

PART A

1. _____   4. _____

2. _____   5. _____

3. _____   6. _____

PART B

1. _____ + _____ = _____

2. _____ + _____ = _____

3. _____ + _____ = _____

4. _____ + _____ = _____

5. _____ + _____ = _____

6. _____ + _____ = _____

PART C

Add these morphographs together.
Some of the words follow the rule about dropping an **e**.

1. give + en   = _____

2. fool + ish + ly   = _____

3. fine + al + ly   = _____

4. store + age   = _____

5. un + shake + en   = _____

6. thought + ful + ly   = _____

7. un + de + feat + ed = _____

8. pre + date + ed   = _____

9. mis + shape + ed   = _____

10. un + drink + able   = _____

11. strength + en + ed = _____

12. wander + ing   = _____

133

Cross out the misspelled words in these sentences.
Then write the words correctly above the crossed-out words.

Have you replased that worthless moter?

Witch small town is the nicest?

PART **E**

1. <u>Watch</u> how you <u>connect</u> the <u>moter</u> to the
   switch. _____

2. She walked <u>nightly</u> <u>thruogh</u> the <u>quiet</u> park. _____

3. The cat was <u>playing</u> and <u>streching</u> on the
   <u>couch</u>. _____

134

LESSON 104

PART A

note   vote   quote

PART B

We heard them try to deny the facts.

_____

_____

PART C

1. _____ + _____ = _____
2. _____ + _____ = _____
3. _____ + _____ = _____
4. _____ + _____ = _____
5. _____ + _____ = _____
6. _____ + _____ = _____

PART D

Circle each short word that ends **cvc**.
Remember: Short words have four letters or less.
      The letter **y** is a vowel letter at the end of a morphograph.

1. skin   3. spin   5. play   7. grab   9. stay   11. slam

2. tray   4. wander   6. person   8. ship   10. fit   12. bar

135

Add these morphographs together.
Some of the words follow the rule about dropping an **e**.

1. quote + able = _____
2. re + fuse + al = _____
3. child + ish + ly = _____
4. store + age = _____
5. sign + al = _____
6. de + sign + er = _____
7. person + able = _____
8. use + ful + ly = _____
9. rise + en = _____
10. un + nerve + ed = _____

1. They <u>hired</u> a <u>likable</u> <u>persen</u> to do the job. _____
2. The <u>athour</u> of the book <u>faced</u> a <u>sizable</u> job. _____
3. Some <u>poeple</u> often <u>misspell</u> <u>words</u>. _____

Lesson 105 is a test lesson. There is no worksheet.

136

LESSON 106

PART A

wreck   wrote   write   wrong   wrap

PART B

__ __ _ e a __ __ __ __ __ __ __ __ y __ __ _ e _ y

__ __ __ __ __ __ __ __ .

_____

_____

PART C

1. _____   5. _____

2. _____   6. _____

3. _____   7. _____

4. _____   8. _____

PART D

Add these morphographs together.
Some of the words follow the rule about doubling
the final **c** in short words.

1. leak + age = _____

2. slip + ed   = _____

3. star + less = _____

4. win + ing   = _____

5. norm + al   = _____

6. flat + en   = _____

7. drip + ed   = _____

8. snug + ly   = _____

137

Draw a line from each word to its clue.

1. whole •   • Have you heard that _____ before?

2. hear •   • _____ vegetable do you like best?

3. here •   • Can you eat a _____ watermelon?

4. tale •   • correct

5. tail •   • putting words on paper

6. which •   • I can _____ you quite well.

7. write •   • Those things belong _____ .

8. right •   • they own it

9. their •   • part of an animal

1. It was <u>pointles</u> to try to <u>repackage</u> the <u>water</u>   _____
   tank.

2. The <u>helpers</u> enjoy <u>careing</u> for older <u>people</u>.   _____

LESSON 107

PART A

source   style   straight   prove

PART B

1. _____

2. _____

PART C

1. W _ _ _ _   4. W _ _ _ _

2. W _ _ _   5. W _ _ _ _

3. W _ _ _ _

PART D

_ _ _ e a _ _   _ _ _ _   _ _ _   _ _   _ _ _ y

_ _ _   _ _ _ _ _ .

_____

_____

PART E

mistaken	pointless	unquotable
previewed	people	stretching
lengthening	equal	golden
valuable	formal	harmlessly
person	resign	faultless
swimmer	lighten	largely

139

Fill in the blanks to show the morphographs in each word.

1. _____ + _____ + _____ = boyishness

2. _____ + _____ + _____ = departed

3. _____ + _____ + _____ = mistaken

4. _____ + _____ + _____ = resigned

5. _____ + _____ + _____ + _____ = unreserved

6. _____ + _____ + _____ = rightfully

7. _____ + _____ + _____ = preplanned

8. _____ + _____ = wreckage

1. I don't <u>beleive</u> that the <u>lightest</u> soft drink is the most <u>refreshing</u>.   _____

2. The <u>unripened</u> bananas were not <u>goldend</u>, but greenish.   _____

140

LESSON 108

PART **A**

1. _____   5. _____

2. _____   6. _____

3. _____   7. _____

4. _____   8. _____

PART **B**

1. _____

2. _____

PART **C**

Add these morphographs together.
Some of the words follow the rule about doubling the final **c**
in short words.

1. play + ful   = _____

2. re + source   = _____

3. spin + ing   = _____

4. style + ish   = _____

5. wrap + er   = _____

6. straight + en + ing = _____

7. re + store   = _____

8. sad + est   = _____

PART D

These words are in the puzzle.
Circle 7 or more of the words.

serving	line	port
berry	plan	voice
sign	game	vote
arm	sell	equal

```
s  g  i  s  i  g  n
s  e  r  v  i  n  g
b  q  l  p  o  o  a
e  u  v  l  o  t  m
r  a  o  a  a  r  e
r  l  i  n  e  r  t
y  v  o  i  c  e  m
```

142

LESSON 109

PART A

1. study
2. pity
3. copy
4. fancy
5. sturdy
6. hurry
7. busy
8. worry
9. story
10. carry
11. glory
12. fury

PART B

1. _____

2. _____

PART C

1. _____
2. _____
3. _____
4. _____
5. _____
6. _____

PART D

Write the word for each meaning.
The words will contain these morphographs:

ish—like

al—related to

en—to make

de—away from, down

ful—full of

pre—before

word	meaning
1. _____	full of hope
2. _____	to make wide
3. _____	press down
4. _____	like a child
5. _____	plan before
6. _____	related to rent

143

Fill in the blanks to show the morphographs in each word.

1. _____ + _____ + _____ = resourceful
2. _____ + _____ = wrapping
3. _____ + _____ = straightest
4. _____ + _____ + _____ = designer
5. _____ + _____ + _____ = reserving
6. _____ + _____ = stopping
7. _____ + _____ = noting
8. _____ + _____ = notable
9. _____ + _____ = used
10. _____ + _____ + _____ = strengthening

PART F

1. Mix the <u>doseage</u> by <u>putting</u> it in a <u>shaker</u>. _____

2. The <u>cheapest</u> <u>packageing</u> may not be <u>sturdy</u>. _____

3. The <u>stylesh</u> <u>speaker</u> will have a <u>starring</u> role. _____

• •

Lesson 110 is a test lesson. There is no worksheet.

144

LESSON 111

© SRA/McGraw-Hill. All rights reserved.

PART A

1. _ o _ _ _
2. _ u _ _
3. _ u r _ _

4. _ _ _ c _
5. _ _ _ _ y
6. _ u s _

7. _ _ _ _ _
8. _ _ _ _ _ _

PART B

Please answer the question.

_____

PART C

PART D

Make 11 real words from the morphographs in the box.

fine	wide	ly	est	bare	quiet	ness

1. _____
2. _____
3. _____
4. _____
5. _____
6. _____

7. _____
8. _____
9. _____
10. _____
11. _____

145

LESSON 112

PART A

date   hate   plate   rate
fate   late   state   skate

PART B

__e a s_   ___w e_   ___   q u__t i o_.

_____

PART C

Add these morphographs together.
Remember: The morphograph **y** is a vowel letter.

1. shine + y = _____   5. spot + y   = _____

2. sleep + y = _____   6. ease + y   = _____

3. noise + y = _____   7. dress + y = _____

4. length + y = _____   8. scare + y = _____

146

Circle the misspelled word in each group.
Then write it correctly in the blank.

1. madnes
   story
   picture
   chalk

   _____

2. design
   reserve
   saddness
   sturdy

   _____

3. heard
   people
   noise
   rong

   _____

4. quietly
   equally
   really
   proove

   _____

5. studey
   straight
   stretch
   strength

   _____

6. several
   packege
   final
   bridge

   _____

LESSON 113

_ _ _ a s _   _ _ _ w _ _   _ _ _   q _ _ _ t i _ _ .

_____

PART B

1. _____   5. _____

2. _____   6. _____

3. _____   7. _____

4. _____   8. _____

PART C

_____

_____

_____

_____

_____

_____

_____

_____

148

Add these morphographs together.
Remember: The morphograph **y** is a vowel letter.

1. ease + y   = _____
2. fool + ish + ly   = _____
3. form + al + ly   = _____
4. store + age   = _____
5. sleep + y   = _____
6. length + y   = _____
7. fate + al   = _____
8. re + source + ful = _____
9. note + able   = _____
10. straight + en   = _____

Fill in the blanks to show the morphographs in each word.

1. _____ + _____ + _____ = designer
2. _____ + _____ + _____ = unplanned
3. _____ + _____ + _____ = strengthening
4. _____ + _____ = maddest
5. _____ + _____ + _____ = related
6. _____ + _____ = wreckage
7. _____ + _____ = really
8. _____ + _____ + _____ = unproven

LESSON 114

PART A

_____ _____ __ _____.

_____

PART B

1. _ k _ _ _   4. _ a _ _

2. _ _ _ _ e   5. _ _ _ _

3. _ l _ _ _

PART C

1. _____   5. _____

2. _____   6. _____

3. _____   7. _____

4. _____   8. _____

Circle the misspelled word in each group.
Then write it correctly in the blank.

1. sleepy
   noisey
   design
   used

   _____

2. easy
   picture
   peeple
   wrapping

   _____

3. bigest
   carry
   quietest
   skillful

   _____

4. cheeper
   source
   fancy
   winning

   _____

5. dripping
   useful
   mistaken
   finaly

   _____

6. delightful
   defeeted
   childish
   golden

   _____

· ·

This is the last worksheet in Level C.
There are no student worksheets for Lessons 115-120.

Word Lists

better
beetle
book
done
enough
friends
good
green
home
keep
listen
little
look
many
meet
need
over
quiet
see
should
shove
some
street
thought
through
took
was
weed
where
wonder

Lesson 5

bright
fight
flight
fright
high
light

meat
might
night
right
talks
than
tight
writes

Lesson 10

ate
bananas
breakfast
cry
fly
for
grandmother
my
shy
sight
sly
try
why

Lesson 15

anybody
ape
cape
clay
didn't
drape
escape
gape
grape
listen
play
scrape
shape

stay
tape

Lesson 20

away
bay
born
corn
day
fork
porch
pork
port
say
sport
today
torch
torn

Lesson 25

bloom
boot
broom
brush
cool
coop
food
fool
hoot
mood
moon
noon
room
scoop
soon
spoon
stoop
them

these
think
troop
want
which
would

Lesson 30

back
believe
clock
every
kick
lock
lost
luck
neck
pack
pick
race
rock
shock
sick
stack
tack
thick
track
trick

Lesson 35

badge
black
bridge
budge
building
deck
dodge
duck

from
fudge
hedge
judge
ledge
lodge
other
people
pledge
ridge
rough
stuck
tough
truck
watched
wood

Lesson 40

bliss
boss
cage
caught
change
class
could
dress
fuss
glass
graceful
hiss
huge
large
loss
mess
nudge
page
press
rowboats
sailboats

152

Word Lists

stage
wage
write

Lesson 45

children
choice
eight
face
fence
grace
lace
left
moss
motor
nice
place
school
since
space
their
together
trace
voice

Lesson 50

act
blackest
build
coldest
count
counting
fresh
greenest
happy
lightest
lighting
listening

pressing
print
quietest
rebuilding
refresh
refreshing
rent
repack
repacking
replace
rest
rethinking
ring
spend
spending
string
thank
undone
unfolding
unhappy
unlocking
unpacking
water
wondering

Lesson 55

author
bike
blame
blue
brownest
coolest
cube
different
dressing
drive
endless
equal

fine
fire
frame
friendless
game
globe
great
ground
harm
helpless
hope
human
joke
lake
leader
make
misplace
misspelling
mistake
name
pine
pipe
point
poke
pure
rage
rake
reach
real
refine
repay
reporting
restless
rewrite
ride
ripe
robe
safe

serve
several
shine
side
skill
smoke
snake
spell
stories
take
there
those
toughest
town
trust
unclear
unkindest
unlock
unmask
unrefreshing
unsound
unthinking
vine
wide
worth
worthless
wrote

Lesson 60

break
chalk
charge
charm
cheap
child
chill
choke
city

cure
feat
helplessness
hire
kindest
length
misjudge
refill
slice
strength
toughness
uneven
unsold
untrusting
value

Lesson 65

above
boundless
breakable
brown
catch
charming
ditch
file
greenness
helped
like
match
misspell
misstep
mistake
needless
notch
portable
quietness
rebuild
refillable

Word Lists

report
restlessness
roughness
round
size
started
stitch
stretch
thoughtless-
ness
unbreakable
unkindness
unsure
unthinkable
unworkable
wanted
washable
witch
workable

Lesson 70

bench
brushing
bunch
changeless
civil
coldness
curable
darkness
feet
fineness
finest
freshest
grounded
hired
hoped
hopeless
hoping

judged
largest
likable
lunch
mismatched
patch
pinch
pitch
pointlessness
prepay
preschool
preshrunk
pretest
preview
purest
racing
remark
repacked
reviewed
ripeness
scratch
search
shameless
shaping
shining
shrunk
sketch
smoking
speech
speechless
staging
switch
teach
touch
unsoundness
usable
useless
using
valuable

valueless
valuing
view
watch
widest
writing

Lesson 75

blameless
careless
clothes
clue
colder
driving
equally
faced
fighter
finer
fresher
friendly
greater
greatness
helper
helplessly
hiring
homeless
hopelessly
joker
judging
know
life
lighter
lightly
likely
likeness
lovable
nameless
new

nicely
placed
previewed
quietly
reformed
remarkable
replaced
reserved
rougher
serving
shame
sizable
soap
stretcher
teacher
time
tracing
twice
unequally
unusable
wash
widely
wideness

Lesson 80

baker
bite
biting
bluest
brightness
caring
catcher
cheaper
fired
goodness
greatest
harmlessly
kite

largely
lifeless
matching
misjudged
namely
needlessly
nightly
parked
picking
pointless
prejudge
preserve
preserving
previewing
probing
pureness
quite
rehiring
renaming
resorted
restlessly
reviewer
searched
searching
sketching
slightest
smell
spite
touching
unequal
unlikely
unpacked
unreachable
unstuck
uselessness
white
whitest
wisely

154

Word Lists

Lesson 85

boldness
changing
choking
civilly
finely
formless
larger
liked
liking
nicer
notable
noted
noting
often
paints
person
pictures
researching
stretchable
stretched
stretching
tale
thoughtlessly
timeless
timely
unbelievable
unlikable
unlike
used
washing
working

Lesson 90

bare
believable
blissful
care

careful
carry
cheapest
choicest
cope
darken
define
deform
deport
depress
deserved
devalue
fault
forceful
freshen
grandest
helpful
hopeful
joking
lengthen
lighten
locker
misused
nicest
redefine
restful
rope
scope
shortly
sign
sing
slope
tail
thickness
unfilling
unrefined
unstuck
watching
whiter

Lesson 95

barred
biggest
blissful
caring
carry
childish
civilly
coil
dealing
decoding
defined
delighted
deserving
design
dropping
farmer
fault
faultless
fineness
fitness
fly
foolish
formal
formless
global
golden
grandly
greenish
hear
herb
hopefully
hopeless
hotly
humanness
maddest
madly
madness

nerve
package
packaging
page
passage
personable
planned
planner
play
point
recoiled
rental
runner
sadden
sadder
saddest
sadly
sadness
shopped
shopper
shopping
signal
snapping
spotted
star
starless
starred
starring
stay
stepping
stopping
swimmer
swimming
talked
tripped
unchanging
unequally
unripened
usage

verb
verbal
wander
washable
watered
watering
weaken
winner
work
world

Lesson 100

barely
bigger
brownish
cheaply
childishly
delightful
deny
designer
dosage
dripless
dripping
dropper
facing
facts
final
finally
flatten
flattest
foolishly
given
heard
here
hottest
misshaped
note
predated

155

Word Lists

putting
quotable
quote
refusal
ripest
risen
running
skipping
slipped
snugly
snugness
spotless
storage
strengthened
taken
thoughtfully
trapped
undefeated
undrinkable
unnerved
unshaken
unsnapped
usefully
vote
wandering
worldly
yardage

boyishness
busy
carry
cheaper
civilly
copy
departed
designer
dripped
dropping
fancy
faultless
flatten
fury
glory
harmlessly
hurry
leakage
misjudged
mistaken
normal
notable
noting
pity
playful

preplanned
previewed
prove
reserving
resigned
resource
resourceful
restore
rightfully
saddest
shaken
skillfully
slightly
slipped
snugly
source
spinning
starless
stopping
storing
story
straight
straightest
strengthening
study
sturdy
style

stylish
unquotable
unreserved
unthinkable
used
valuable
whole
winning
worry
wrap
wrapper
wrapping
wreck
wreckage
wrong

answer
bareness
barest
cloudy
dressy
easy
fatal
formally
hate

hole
late
lengthy
mighty
misquoted
noisy
picture
plate
please
question
rate
really
related
reserve
scary
shiny
skate
sleepy
speaker
spotty
state
unplanned
unproven
unwrap

Spelling Rules

Lesson 71	**Final E Rule**	When do you drop the **e** from a word?
		When the next morphograph begins with a vowel letter.
Lesson 91	**Doubling Rule**	When do you double the final **c** in a short word?
		When the word ends **cvc** and the next morphograph begins with **v.**
Lesson 101	**Y as a Vowel**	When is **y** a vowel letter?
		At the end of a morphograph.

Meanings of Prefixes and Suffixes

Morphograph	Lesson	Meanings	Examples
-able	66	(able to be)	stretchable, washable
-al	98	(related to, like)	formal, trial, rental
-age	96	(that which is, state)	package, usage, marriage
de-	91	(down, away from)	deport, deform, describe
-ed	69	(in the past)	stepped, cried, wooded
-en	94	(make)	loosen, bitten, proven
-er	76	(more; one who)	easier, lighter, trapper
-est	54	(the most)	lightest, happiest
-ful	92	(full of)	careful, forgetful, beautiful
-ing	51	(when you do something)	spending, moving, stopping
-ish	99	(like, related to; to make)	babyish, selfish, finish
-less	57	(without)	painless, useless, restless
-ly	77	(how something is)	equally, basically, motherly
mis-	58	(wrong)	misspell, mistrial, misprint
-ness	64	(that which is)	thickness, uselessness
pre-	73	(before)	preview, preclude, prepay
re-	51	(again, back)	rerun, return, replace
un-	53	(not, the opposite)	unhappy, unusual, untie
-y	111	(having the quality of; in the manner of; small)	shiny, activity, doggy

157

Test Charts

	Lesson 5	Lesson 10	Lesson 15	Lesson 20	Lesson 25	Lesson 30	30 Lesson Total
Super Speller	25	25	25	25	25	25	
	24	24	24	24	24	24	
Very Good Speller	23	23	23	23	23	23	138 = *Super Speller*
	22	22	22	22	22	22	
	21	21	21	21	21	21	
	20	20	20	20	20	20	
	19	19	19	19	19	19	
	18	18	18	18	18	18	
	17	17	17	17	17	17	
	16	16	16	16	16	16	
	15	15	15	15	15	15	
	14	14	14	14	14	14	
	13	13	13	13	13	13	
	12	12	12	12	12	12	
	11	11	11	11	11	11	
	10	10	10	10	10	10	
	9	9	9	9	9	9	
	8	8	8	8	8	8	
	7	7	7	7	7	7	
	6	6	6	6	6	6	
	5	5	5	5	5	5	
	4	4	4	4	4	4	
	3	3	3	3	3	3	
	2	2	2	2	2	2	
	1	1	1	1	1	1	

Test Charts

	Lesson 35	Lesson 40	Lesson 45	Lesson 50	Lesson 55	Lesson 60	30 Lesson Total
	25	25	25	25	25	25	
Super Speller	24	24	24	24	24	24	
	23	23	23	23	23	23	138 = *Super Speller*
Very Good Speller	22	22	22	22	22	22	
	21	21	21	21	21	21	
	20	20	20	20	20	20	
	19	19	19	19	19	19	
	18	18	18	18	18	18	
	17	17	17	17	17	17	
	16	16	16	16	16	16	
	15	15	15	15	15	15	
	14	14	14	14	14	14	
	13	13	13	13	13	13	
	12	12	12	12	12	12	
	11	11	11	11	11	11	
	10	10	10	10	10	10	
	9	9	9	9	9	9	
	8	8	8	8	8	8	
	7	7	7	7	7	7	
	6	6	6	6	6	6	
	5	5	5	5	5	5	
	4	4	4	4	4	4	
	3	3	3	3	3	3	
	2	2	2	2	2	2	
	1	1	1	1	1	1	

Test Charts

	Lesson 65	Lesson 70	Lesson 75	Lesson 80	Lesson 85	Lesson 90	30 Lesson Total
	25	25	25	25	25	25	
Super Speller	24	24	24	24	24	24	
	23	23	23	23	23	23	138 = *Super Speller*
Very Good Speller	22	22	22	22	22	22	
	21	21	21	21	21	21	
	20	20	20	20	20	20	
	19	19	19	19	19	19	
	18	18	18	18	18	18	
	17	17	17	17	17	17	
	16	16	16	16	16	16	
	15	15	15	15	15	15	
	14	14	14	14	14	14	
	13	13	13	13	13	13	
	12	12	12	12	12	12	
	11	11	11	11	11	11	
	10	10	10	10	10	10	
	9	9	9	9	9	9	
	8	8	8	8	8	8	
	7	7	7	7	7	7	
	6	6	6	6	6	6	
	5	5	5	5	5	5	
	4	4	4	4	4	4	
	3	3	3	3	3	3	
	2	2	2	2	2	2	
	1	1	1	1	1	1	

160

Test Charts

	Lesson 95	Lesson 100	Lesson 105	Lesson 110	Lesson 115	Lesson 120	30 Lesson Total
Super Speller	25	25	25	25	25	25	
	24	24	24	24	24	24	138 = **Super Speller**
Very Good Speller	23	23	23	23	23	23	
	22	22	22	22	22	22	
	21	21	21	21	21	21	
	20	20	20	20	20	20	
	19	19	19	19	19	19	
	18	18	18	18	18	18	
	17	17	17	17	17	17	
	16	16	16	16	16	16	
	15	15	15	15	15	15	
	14	14	14	14	14	14	
	13	13	13	13	13	13	
	12	12	12	12	12	12	
	11	11	11	11	11	11	
	10	10	10	10	10	10	
	9	9	9	9	9	9	
	8	8	8	8	8	8	
	7	7	7	7	7	7	
	6	6	6	6	6	6	
	5	5	5	5	5	5	
	4	4	4	4	4	4	
	3	3	3	3	3	3	
	2	2	2	2	2	2	
	1	1	1	1	1	1	